Drawing Dinosaurs
and other
Prehistoric Animals

Don Bolognese
Drawing Dinosaurs
and other
Prehistoric Animals

FRANKLIN WATTS
New York   London   Toronto   Sydney
1982

Library of Congress Cataloging in Publication Data

Bolognese, Don.

Drawing dinosaurs and other prehistoric animals.

(How-to-draw book)
Summary: Outlines the fundamentals of
drawing dinosaurs and other prehistoric
creatures from fossils, models, and toys.
1. Dinosaurs in art — Juvenile literature.
2. Mammals, Fossil, in art — Juvenile literature. 3. Drawing — Technique. [1. Dinosaurs
in art. 2. Mammals, Fossil, in art.
3. Animal painting and illustration.
4. Drawing — Technique] I. Title. II. Series.
NC780.5.B6   743'.6   81-23130
ISBN 0-531-04398-3   AACR2

The illustrations on the following pages were
drawn at the American Museum of Natural History,
New York City:

pages 8, 12 (top), 13, 14,
24, 25, 26-27, 28, 29,
33 (bottom), 34, 36,
40 (top), 62, 63,
and 66 (top).

CONTENTS

To Tommy, Craig, and
all other dinosaur lovers

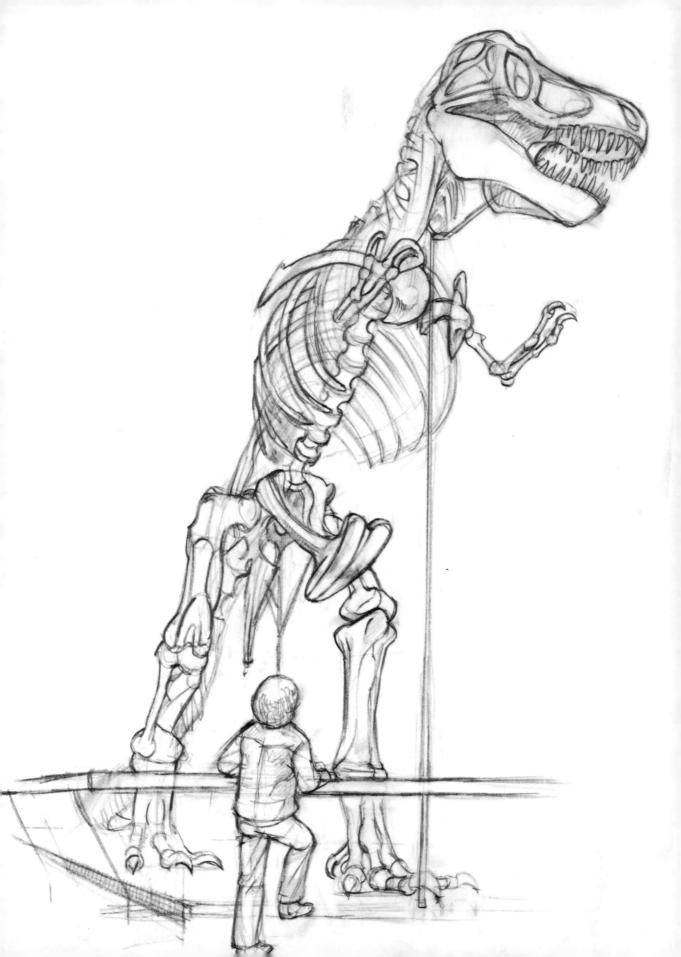

INTRODUCTION

You are standing in a museum. Towering above
you is the fossilized skeleton of a creature that
lived a long time ago. The bones have turned to
stone after being buried for millions of years.
Now scientists have painstakingly put the bones
back together. As you stare up at the animal, try
to imagine what life was like millions of years
ago.

Suddenly, the space you are standing in
becomes a time machine. Dials light up, comput-
ers spin, the machine is taking you back, back
through time: one million, two million years.
The time clock is clicking faster and faster. You
can barely read the dates: 20 million, 30 million
B.C. Now the clock reads 50 million B.C. The
machine slows down. You look at the dial. The
numbers stop changing. The dial reads 60 million
B.C.

There is no sound. You look around. The
museum is gone. In its place is a tropical forest.
Strange, giant ferns grow on all sides. You
look up. Twenty feet above you, its huge jaws
open, is *Tyrannosaurus rex*. You see every
detail. The scaly skin, the daggerlike teeth, and
the snakelike eyes look straight at you.

Frantically, hoping you hit the right button,
you punch in a date. Lights glow, the time
machine whirs and spins and whisks you back,
back to the safety of the museum. Cautiously

9

you look up. *Tyrannosaurus rex* is still there, but only in its skeleton form. People walk by studying this interesting relic of the past. They don't know what a narrow escape you've just had. If only you could recreate that long-ago tropical scene so that you would be able to capture permanently what you have just experienced. If you could do that in pictures, then you would be doing what artists have done for thousands of years.

Stegosaurus skeleton

Toy dinosaurs

CHAPTER 1
Getting Started

Drawing dinosaurs is very simple. There are no tricks or formulas to memorize. You will have to learn to *look* very carefully. And you will have to practice drawing until the pencil in your hand does what you want it to do.

Basically, there are two ways to practice.

First, there is *sketching*. Sketches are really quick drawings. Usually they are done in a few minutes or even seconds. They can express movements, gestures, and moods. Sketching trains your eyes and hand to be alert and quick.

Allosaurus claw

Second, there is the *drawing study*. This kind of drawing requires more time. It can sometimes take hours. But it will train you to see *more* and to see it more *carefully*. It will help you to understand the true form and structure of your subject.

For example, the sketch of the *Allosaurus* claws shows us a feeling of its shape and position. The drawing study, however, gives us more information. We see how the bones fit together. We can almost feel the sharp claws.

Now you will need something to sketch and draw from. We know that there are no dinosaurs in zoos or in forests, so you must search elsewhere for references. The drawings in this book will be a great help to you, but there are other sources you should know about.

FOSSILS

Many museums have fossilized remains of dinosaurs and other prehistoric animals (see the list on page 70). These displays are particularly good models for studying skeletons. They will also give you a better sense of the true size of these creatures. The most accomplished painters of prehistoric scenes use such models as studies for their drawings or paintings.

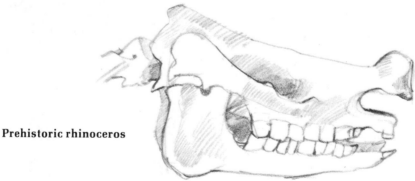

Prehistoric rhinoceros

BOOKS AND PICTURES

Collect as many pictures as you can of dinosaur scenes showing the trees and other surroundings that existed during the dinosaur age. This will help you understand the set-

Toy dinosaurs

tings for your drawings. Start a collection of pictures that show all kinds of dinosaurs in different positions and from many angles.

TOYS AND MODELS

Toy dinosaurs can be very useful as models for drawing. As you will see in the next chapter, they can be used to create a miniature scene. This scene can then be the model for a dramatic picture.

LIVE CREATURES

Lizards and other small amphibians have many features that are similar to those of dinosaurs. You can find them in pet stores or at zoos. Look especially for such details as the skin, the eyes, and the tail.

Chameleon

ART SUPPLIES

Pencils—An ordinary no. 2 pencil is fine for a beginning. Later you will want a wider range of tones. These should go from H (medium light) through the Bs (HB, B 2B, 3B) up to the soft and dark 4B. You will also need a pencil sharpener and a sandpaper block for extra fine points.

Felt pens—water-soluble ones with fine points.

Erasers—Use a kneaded eraser for small areas. To lighten pencil strokes, just press the eraser without rubbing. The eraser will lift off the pencil marks you don't want. Plastic erasers are superior to gum erasers for large areas. Erasers are not only for correcting mistakes. They are a useful tool for getting highlights in shaded areas.

Paper—Any good drawing paper will do, unless it's rough in texture or too thin. Tracing paper can be used for sketching, but too much erasing will tear it.

Clips—Clips are necessary for holding pads together, especially when you are drawing in museums.

Lightbox for tracing—Working up your drawing through the sketch phase to a more finished picture can be much easier with a lightbox. The simplest lightbox is a window with light coming through. Tape a drawing to the window. Then tape a fresh paper over the drawing and trace. If the paper is too thick, the light will not go through it. A simple desk top lightbox can be made by putting pieces of glass (frosted, if possible) in a frame built up enough so that a light bulb can be placed beneath it.

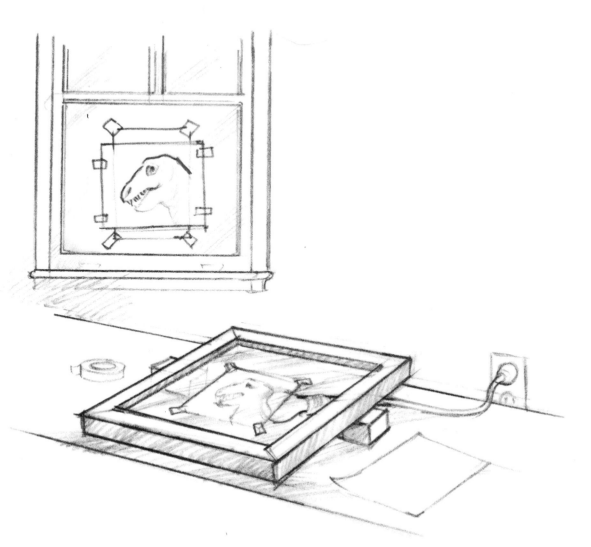

CHAPTER 2
Drawing Step by Step

SKETCHING

Here's a good way to begin. Take out all of your favorite dinosaur pictures. Spread them out on a table or pin them up on the walls. If you have any toy or model dinosaurs, set them up around you. Look through this book and pick out some pictures that interest you. Now, pick up a pencil and sketch pad. Start sketching the dinosaur that appeals most to you. Keep the sketch loose (see A). Just try to capture the shape, position, and attitude of the creature. Don't worry about details. Do several sketches. When you have one that you like, add some trees and ferns (see B). Now you have a setting for your dinosaur. Does it seem to be too ordinary? Try sketching another dinosaur (see C). Use softer pencils (2B to 4B) to add some shading. What is happening to your sketch? It is becoming a picture, with a story and drama. Working this way supplies you with many studies for larger and more detailed pictures. The next few pages illustrate more ways to practice this method of sketching.

MOVEMENT

Here are several points to
look for when you are trying
to capture the posture of
a dinosaur:

- The line from the tail, along the
  back to the neck and up to
  the head.
- The position of the legs. Which legs
  are supporting the weight? If the
  dinosaur is standing on two legs,
  how is it balanced?
- The role of the tail. Don't
  forget that in these creatures
  the tail is very important
  to their stability.

Mosasaur

SIZE

Sketch B on page 18 added foliage. This
created a setting for the dinosaur. It also gave
us an idea of the true size of this animal.
The sketch of *Mosasaur* (above) shows
another example that lets us make a size
comparison.

LIGHT AND DARK

Sketch C
on page 18 shows
how simply you
can create drama
in a picture by
adding dark areas. In
the sketch (right),
shading defines a
specific setting, and even suggests a time of
day. The sense of form and weight in the
illustration to the left is also achieved
through shading. And in the picture below,
dark shading helps to create a feeling of danger.

Tyrannosaurus rex

SKETCHING FROM TOYS AND MODELS

One of the best reasons for sketching directly from toys is the opportunity it gives you to choose different points of view. One minute you are flying low over the outstretched neck of *Tyrannosaurus rex*. The next minute you can be flat on the ground as a monstrous *Brontosaurus* rambles through the forest.

Brontosaurus

Another way to use toy dinosaurs is as part of a miniature scene. Set two or three dinosaur models on a table. Use your picture collection as a guide to the arrangement. Add a few rocks and some plants stuck in clay. Put the setup near a window or put a light just above and to one side, and you will have a typical day in prehistoric times.

Dinosaur models

DRAWING FROM DINOSAUR FOSSILS

When you draw in a museum or in other public places, remember to bring along the following supplies:

- Several sharpened pencils and one or two felt pens
- An eraser
- A small pocket pencil sharpener
- A plastic bag for pencil sharpenings and crumpled papers
- A folding stool, if possible.

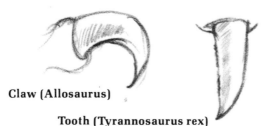

Claw (Allosaurus)

Tooth (Tyrannosaurus rex)

When you first attempt a drawing of a fossil, start with either a small, simple fossil or a part of a larger one. See the examples here of a claw, a tooth, or a leg bone.

As you study and draw the fossilized bones, notice how they are attached to one another. Careful and close observation *now* will help you *later* when you attempt drawing more complicated fossils.

Leg bones (Stegosaurus)

Sometimes, entire creatures with skin and features intact become fossils. If any of these are available, make certain you draw them. Their details and textures will give your drawings a lifelike quality.

Two protoceratops hatching

You started with small pieces of a fossil. Now it's time to put the pieces together and go on to bigger things!

This is a drawing of an *Allosaurus* skeleton that is on display at the American Museum of Natural History in New York City. Drawings like this require careful study and take several hours to do. It is very good practice to draw this way as often as you

Hipbone

Tail

can. The lifelike position of the creature helps you to imagine how the animal really lived. And the close look at its anatomy gives you a better idea of how it moved about.

At the bottom of page 33, there is another sketch of this same animal from the same display. That one is shown from a different angle and was sketched much more quickly.

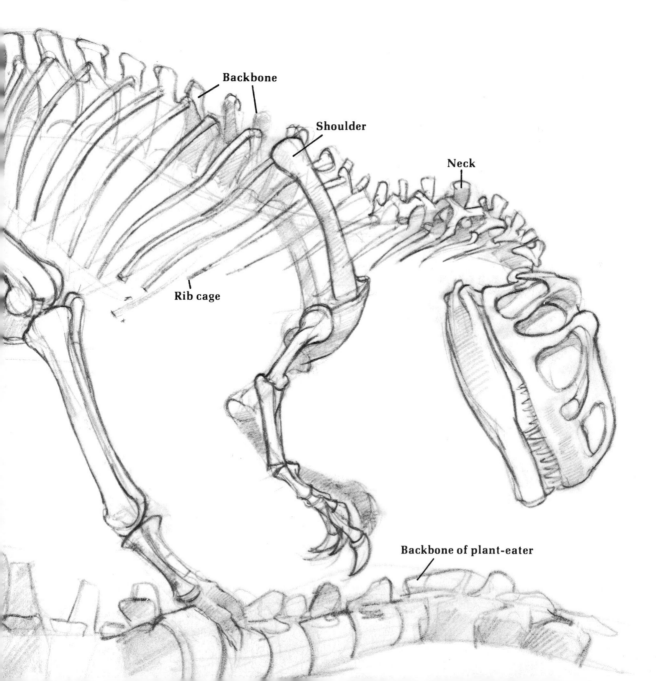

Backbone

Shoulder

Neck

Rib cage

Backbone of plant-eater

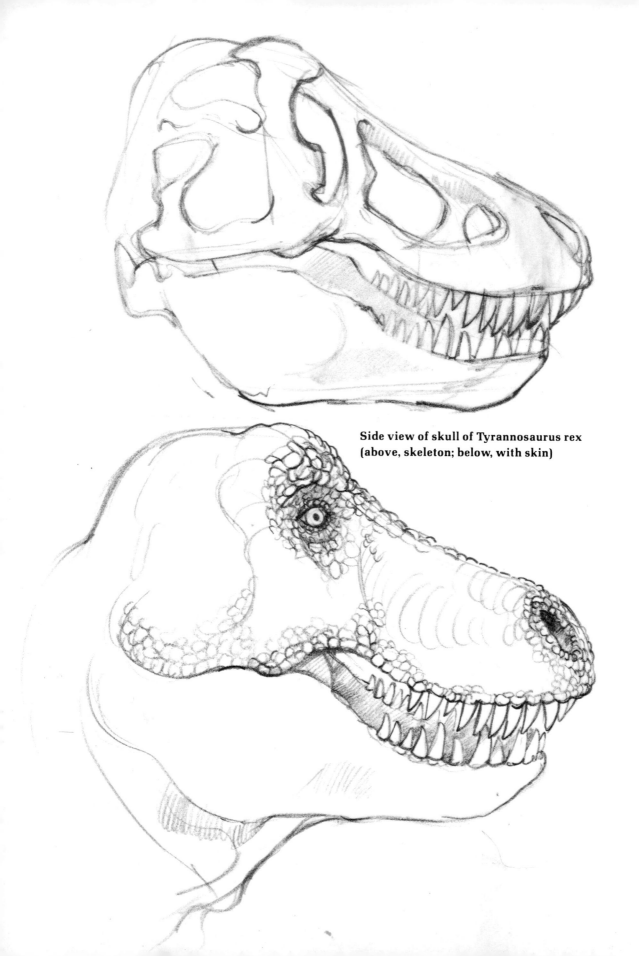

Side view of skull of Tyrannosaurus rex
(above, skeleton; below, with skin)

CHAPTER 3
Dinosaurs in Detail

What makes dinosaurs so exciting? Different answers may come to mind. You may find them "big," "strange," "ferocious," or "horrible." These are the qualities you should try to put into your drawings.

Look at *Tyrannosaurus rex*: big, frightening, and terrifying! In your drawings of the animal, emphasize the features that bring out these qualities. Take the head, for example. It is 4 feet (1.2 m) long and has huge jaws. There are over fifty daggerlike teeth, some of which are 6 inches (15 cm) long.

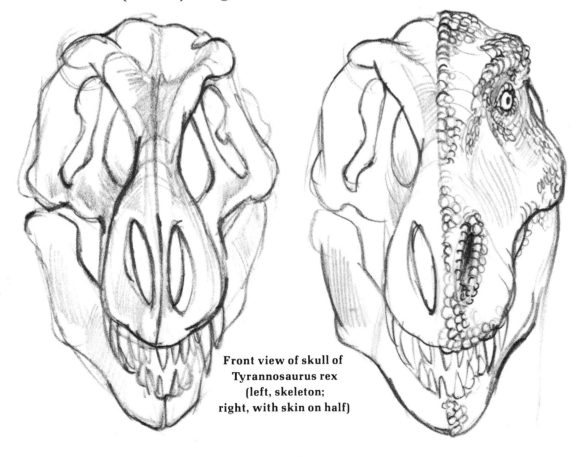

Front view of skull of Tyrannosaurus rex (left, skeleton; right, with skin on half)

Tyrannosaurus rex

Try several quick sketches of *Tyrannosaurus rex* in different positions. Remember that the tail gives the animal its balance. Note how the head, with its sharp teeth, is always the center of interest.

After you have practiced drawing *Tyrannosaurus rex* alone, you might want to show it stalking and attacking its prey.

Tyrannosaurus rex

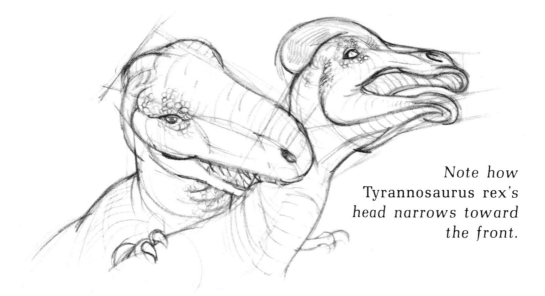

Note how Tyrannosaurus rex's head narrows toward the front.

Tyrannosaurus rex probably used its huge hind feet and claws to attack its victims. But its teeth were its most useful weapon.

A quick sketch of Allosaurus *eating a victim*

Horns and armor on animals are wonderful to draw. And of all the creatures that have ever lived, dinosaurs like *Triceratops* had more of these than any other animal.

This drawing adds skin and features to the skeleton shown at the left. See how closely the completed head matches the skull.

This front view of *Triceratops* is divided down the middle to show how the skeleton looks before and after the skin is added. Put tracing paper over the left side of the drawing and complete it so that it looks like the right side.

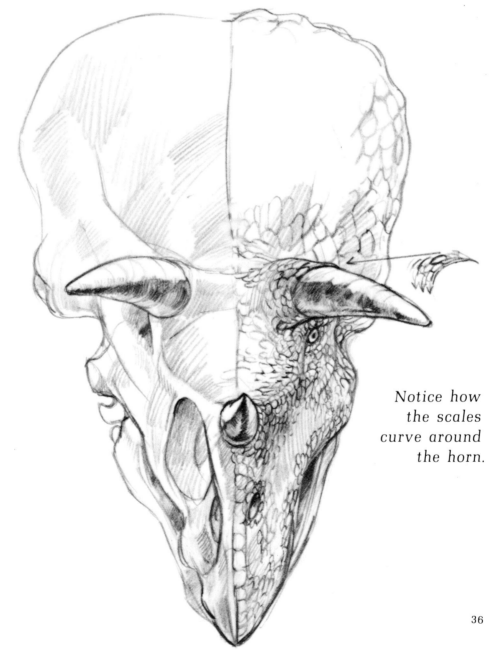

Notice how the scales curve around the horn.

Usually, these dinosaurs were bulky and slow-moving. They depended on their protective armor to defend themselves against large predators like *Tyrannosaurus rex*.

*Note emphasis
on roundness*

Most dinosaurs had longer hind legs than front legs. Even dinosaurs such as *Triceratops* and *Brontosaurus* that walk on all four legs retained longer hind legs.

Note how perspective makes the head appear smaller.

A battle between *Triceratops* and *Tyrannosaurus rex*. Each one is using its most effective defense—*Tyrannosaurus rex*'s teeth and *Triceratops*'s horns.

Styracosaurus

Triceratops had many relatives. Styracosaurus was one of the more unusual ones. It must have been very difficult for a predator like Tyrannosaurus rex to attack Styracosaurus head on!

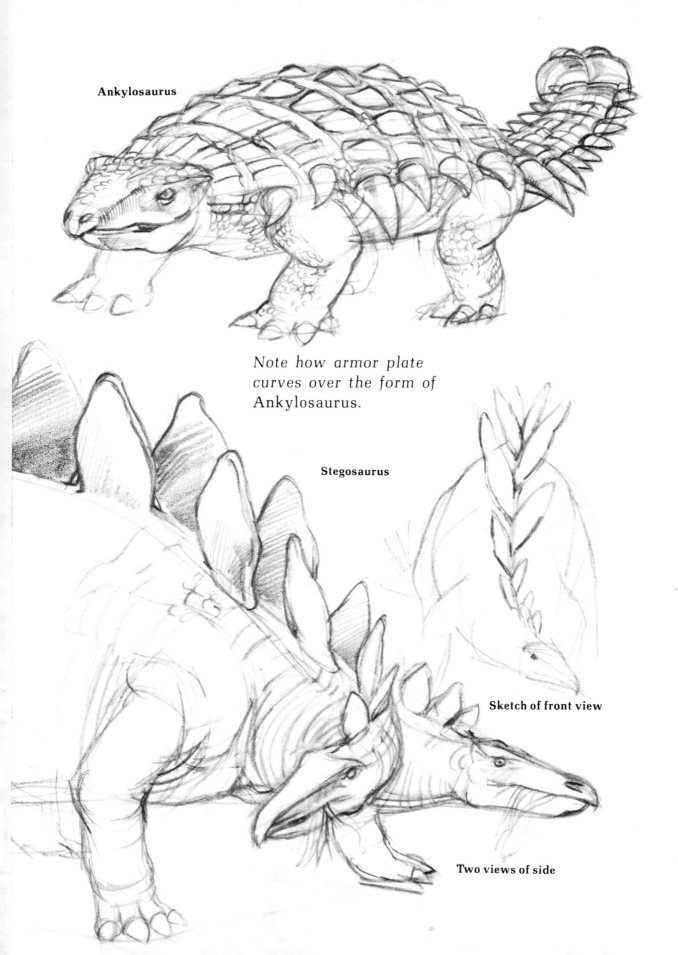

Ankylosaurus

Note how armor plate curves over the form of Ankylosaurus.

Stegosaurus

Sketch of front view

Two views of side

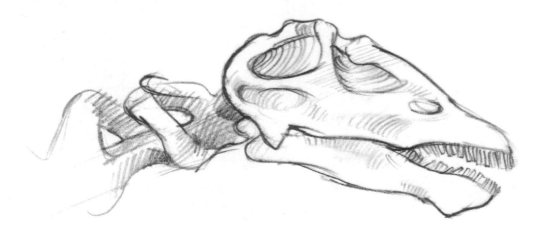

The skull above has recently been recognized as the correct one for *Brontosaurus*. The head that people thought for so long belonged to *Brontosaurus* really came from another plant eater. Below, *Brontosaurus* (with its new head) munches on water plants.

The large plant eaters were a strange combination of forms: large, rounded bodies; trunklike legs; long tails; and thin necks topped by tiny heads. The contrast between all these parts is what you should concentrate on in drawings of these creatures.

This drawing of *Diplodocus* allows us to compare it to the size of a person or a tree.

Note how the form is made rounder by shading.

Brontosaurus

The very simple drawing above can be made more dramatic with shading that follows the form of the neck. Notice the short, dark strokes that create a highlight along the top of the neck. The technique also increases the sense of foreshortening—the illusion that a form is coming toward you.

Notice how firmly *Brachiosaurus* is standing on its treelike legs. Its nostrils, placed high on the skull, enabled it to remain almost completely under water.

This group of dinosaurs was both duck-billed and web-footed. These are some of the most unusual ones. Notice how shading strengthens the form.

Corythosaurus

They also had unusual skull crests. There are several theories about the use of the crests. One is that they allowed for storage of air. Another theory claims that these crests produced honking sounds that might have been mating calls. Whatever their purpose, these crests are fun to draw.

Parasaurolophus

Lambeosaurus

The simple sketch captures the proportion
and position of *Pteranodon.* Remember, details
should only be added
after you are satisfied
with the basic drawing.

The texture of the wing membrane
is done with soft tones of shading.
Use your pencil point for the hairlike
texture on the body.

CHAPTER 4
Flying and Swimming Reptiles

These flying reptiles must have been some of
the strangest looking creatures that ever lived.
Can you imagine one landing on your roof?
One interesting detail about flying reptiles is that
they had hair instead of scales on their bodies.

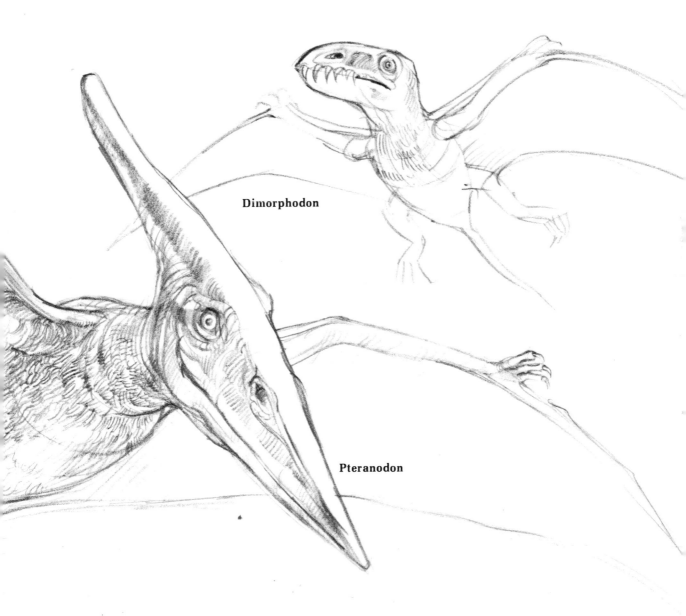

Dimorphodon

Pteranodon

These two pages illustrate how a scene is made more natural by including two or more creatures in the picture.

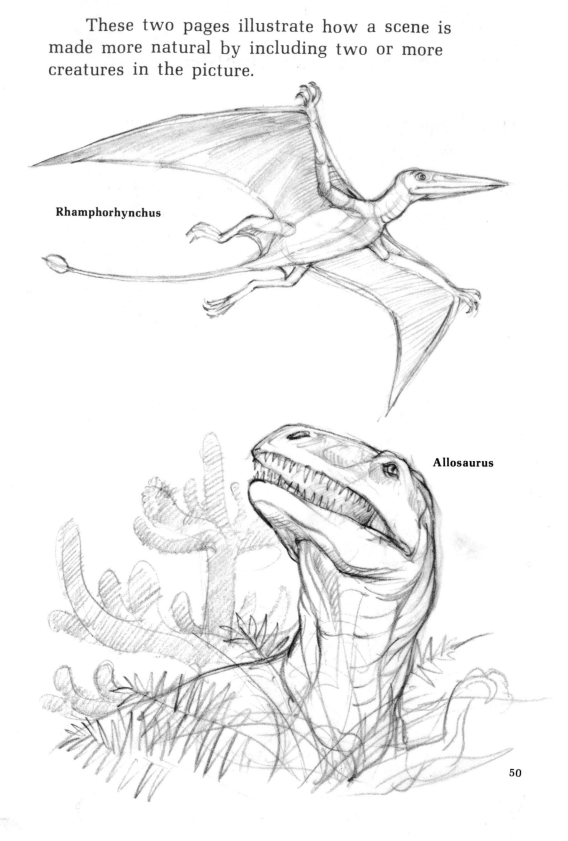

Rhamphorhynchus

Allosaurus

Note how, when
they are perched,
these flying reptiles
resemble four-footed
animals rather than birds.

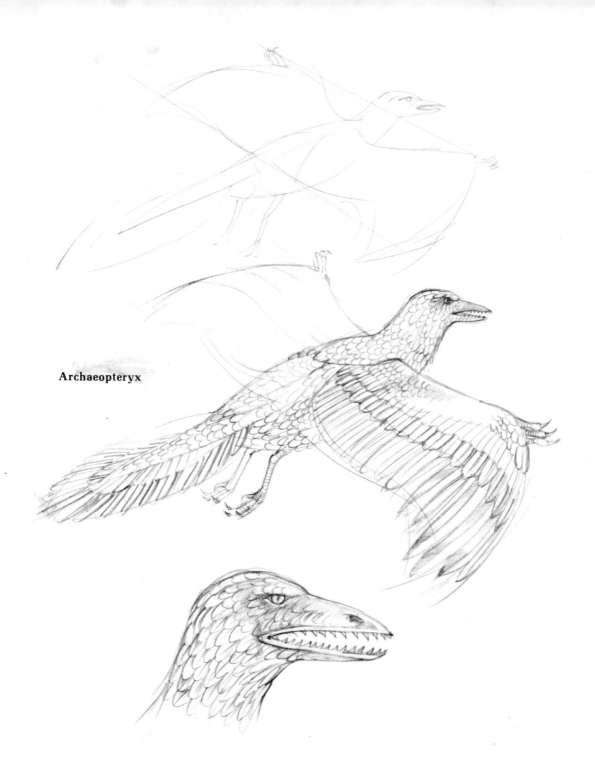

Archaeopteryx

Archaeopteryx, an early type of bird, had feathers. Before adding the feathers, put in guide lines.

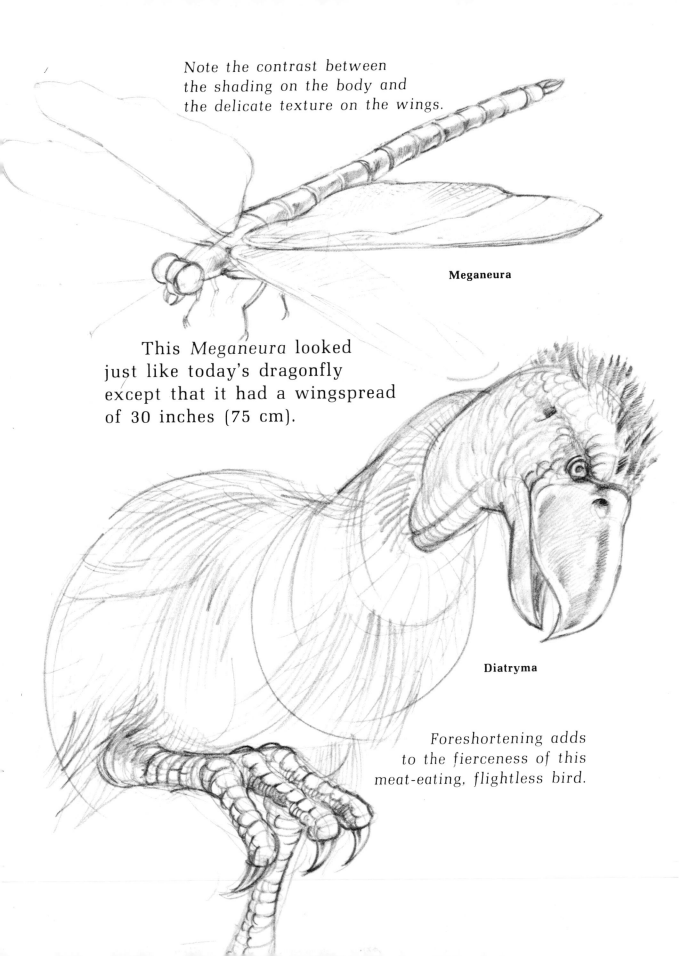

Note the contrast between
the shading on the body and
the delicate texture on the wings.

Meganeura

This *Meganeura* looked
just like today's dragonfly
except that it had a wingspread
of 30 inches (75 cm).

Diatryma

Foreshortening adds
to the fierceness of this
meat-eating, flightless bird.

Rhamphorhynchus

Plesiosaur

54

During the time that dinosaurs ruled the land, there was a group of reptiles that ruled the sea. Some of these grew to tremendous size. *Kronosaurus*, for example, was nearly 50 feet (15.2 m) long. On the next four pages are some instructions that will help to make your drawings of these creatures more fishlike.

Kronosaurus

Flowing lines are essential when you draw underwater creatures. The creatures should always appear to be in motion.

Ichthyosaur

Examples of how shading creates a
streamlined and shiny surface.

Mosasaur

57

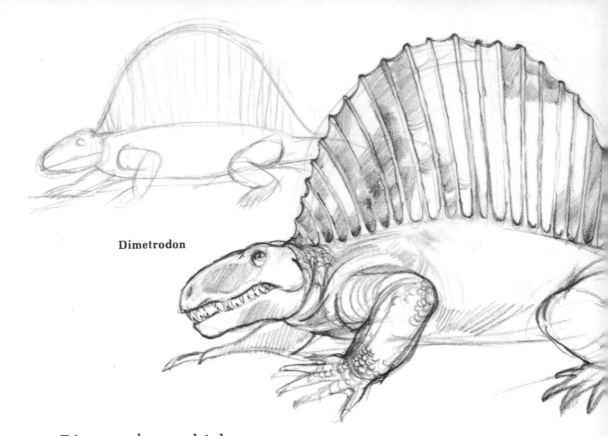

Dimetrodon

Dimetrodon, which lived about 270 million years ago, had a sail on its back. Some scientists think that this was a form both of air conditioning and heating. With its large surface, the sail could either collect heat from the sun or release extra heat in the shade. Whatever its purpose, it provides the artist with a wonderful opportunity for drawing.

Phytosaur

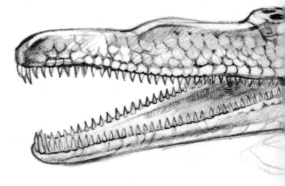

When adding scales and armor, follow the basic form of the animal. For example, note how the scales on *Phytosaur*'s legs turn around and under as they cover the form. A reminder—don't begin adding scales and other details until the basic drawing is complete.

Notice how the sloth walked. Stress the soft, round forms.

**Megatherium
(Giant Grand Sloth)**

CHAPTER 5
Mammals

As dinosaurs became extinct, new types of animals—warm-blooded ones—were taking their place. Although these animals also eventually disappeared, some of them were the ancestors of mammals that live today.

Many of the early mammals were as unusual looking as the dinosaurs. Here are a few of the strangest—and best-known—of them.

Note how Glyptodon's bumps follow the curve of the shell.

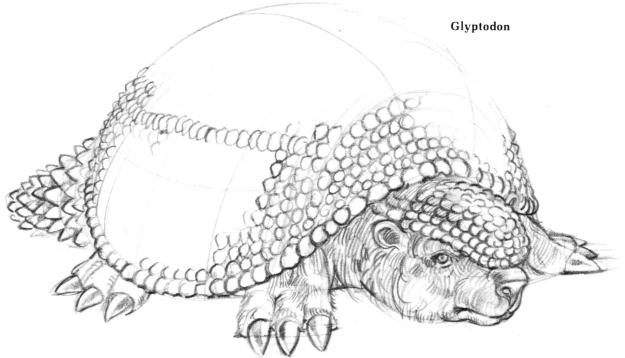

Glyptodon

Unitatherium

Although these two creatures
looked like distant relatives
of the rhinoceros, they
weren't. But they do
provide us with a chance
to draw as many horns
as possible.

Brontotherium

Emphasize the horns
and the tusks. That is the
way to approach the
mammals on these two pages.

Platybelodon

Great Irish Deer

About 15 million years ago, this creature lived in southern Asia and Africa. This ape may have walked on two legs. It had teeth that closely resembled ours. Because of these reasons, some scientists believe this creature might have been the ancestor of human beings.

When we look at today's beautiful horses, it is hard to believe that they descended from the small three- and four-toed creatures that lived over fifty million years ago.

Mesohippus

Eohippus

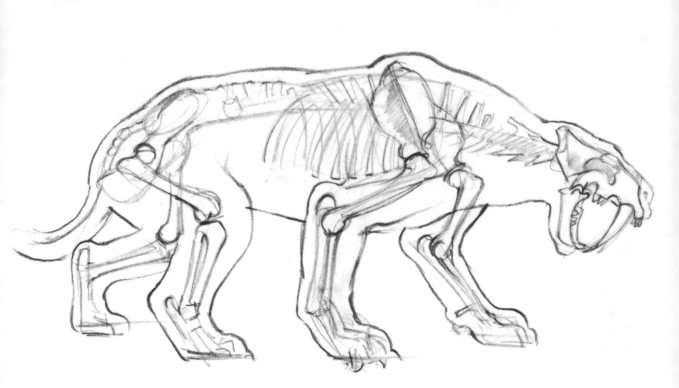

This drawing of a fossil skeleton provides
a good foundation for doing many studies of
the saber-toothed tiger. Note the simple lines
around the skeleton that show the actual
contour of the animal. Keep guide lines loose
and sketchy to increase the feeling of motion.

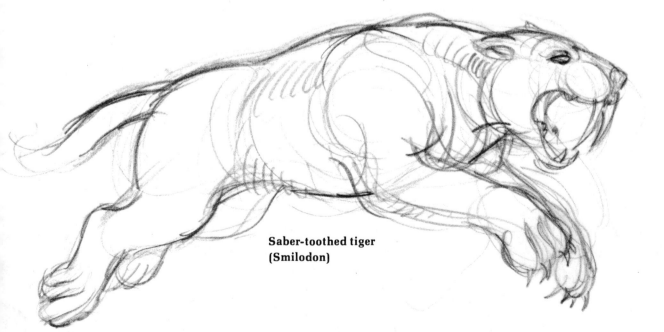

**Saber-toothed tiger
(Smilodon)**

Note how shading with dark accents makes this face more dramatic. See how the cat's claws grasp its victim.

Saber-toothed tiger attacking a sloth

The woolly mammoth, ancestor of today's elephant. Below is a scene that must have happened many times in prehistory. The huge beast is falling victim to the most successful predator that has ever lived: man.

Places to See Dinosaur Fossils

Academy of Natural Sciences, Philadelphia, PA 19103
American Museum of Natural History, New York, NY
    10024
Calgary Zoological Society, Calgary, Alberta
Cleveland Museum of Natural History, Cleveland, OH
    44106
Dallas Museum of Natural History, Dallas, TX 75226
Denver Museum of Natural History, Denver, CO 80825
Dinosaur National Monument, Vernal, UT
Field Museum of Natural History, Chicago, IL 60605
McGill University Museums (Redpath Museum),
    Montreal, Quebec
Museum of Comparative Zoology, Harvard University,
    Cambridge, MA 02138
Museum of Natural History, San Diego, CA 92112
Museum of Natural History (Los Angeles County),
    Los Angeles, CA 90007
Museum of Natural History and Science, Louisville,
    KY 40202
Museum of Science and Natural History, St. Louis,
    MO 63105
National Museum of Canada (Natural History
    Museum), Ottawa, Ontario
National Museum of Natural History, Washington, DC
    20560
Peabody Museum of Natural History, New Haven, CT
    06520
Royal Ontario Museum (University of Toronto),
    Toronto, Ontario
University of British Columbia Geological Museum,
    Vancouver, British Columbia
University of Wisconsin Zoological Museum, Madison,
    WI 53706
Utah Museum of Natural History, Salt Lake City, UT
    84112

About the Author

Don Bolognese is both the author and artist of a dozen books for young readers and has illustrated over 150 books for children and adults. He is a well-known painter, graphic designer, and calligrapher.

A graduate of the Cooper Union Art School, Mr. Bolognese developed and taught a comprehensive course on the art of the book at Cooper Union, Pratt Institute, and New York University. He has won awards from the American Institute of Graphic Arts, the Bologna Bookfair, the Society of Illustrators, and many others.

He and his wife, author/artist Elaine Raphael, make their home in Landgrove, Vermont.

DATE DUE

AUG. 3 1982	AUG 6 1985	NOV 16 1991	
MAR 31 1983	AUG 22 1985	JAN 11 1992	
APR 16 1983	SEP 5	FEB 5 1992	
MAY 17 1983	OCT 1 1985	NOV 05 1992	
JUL 9	DEC 18 1985	JUL 14 1992	
JUL 23 1983	FEB 22 1986	OCT 24	
FEB 3 1984	MAR 21 1986	MAR 29	
FEB 9 1984	APR 25 1986	SEP 23 1997	
JUL 25 1984	JAN 9 1987	AUG 27	
JAN 31 1985	JAN 26 1989		
MAR 20 1985	MAY 11 1989		
MAY 2 1985	AUG 31 1991		
JUL 2 1985			

GAYLORD   PRINTED IN U.S.A.